Francis Hopkinson Smith, Oliver Wendell Holmes, George
Wharton Edwards

The Last Leaf

Poems

Francis Hopkinson Smith, Oliver Wendell Holmes, George Wharton Edwards

The Last Leaf
Poems

ISBN/EAN: 9783337005832

Printed in Europe, USA, Canada, Australia, Japan

Cover: Foto ©Thomas Meinert / pixelio.de

More available books at **www.hansebooks.com**

THE LAST LEAF

POEM

BY

Oliver Wendell Holmes

ILLUSTRATED BY

GEORGE WHARTON EDWARDS

&

F. HOPKINSON SMITH

HOUGHTON MIFFLIN & CO
THE RIVERSIDE PRESS CAMBRIDGE MDCCCXCV

LIST OF ILLUSTRATIONS

LIST of ILLUSTRATIONS

List of Illustrations

THE·LAST·LEAF·

I SAW him once before
As he passed by the door,
      And again
The pavement stones resound,
As he totters o'er the ground
      With his cane.

They say that in his prime,
Ere the pruning-knife of Time
      Cut him down,
Not a better man was found
By the crier on his round
      Through the town.

But now he walks the streets,
And he looks at all he meets,
      Sad and wan,
And he shakes his feeble head,
That it seems as if he said
      "They are gone!"

The Last Leaf ~
~ Continued ~

The mossy marbles rest
On the lips that he has prest
        In their bloom,
And the names he loved to hear
Have been carved for many a year
        On the tomb.

My grandmamma has said —
Poor old lady, she is dead
        Long ago, —
That he had a Roman nose;
And his cheek was like a rose
        In the snow.

But now his nose is thin,
And it rests upon his chin
        Like a staff,
And a crook is in his back,
And a melancholy crack
        In his laugh.

The
LAST:Leaf:
(Conclvded)

I know it is a sin
For me to sit and grin
   At him here,
But the old three-cornered hat
And the breeches, and all that
   Are so queer!

And if I should live to be
The last leaf upon the tree
   In the Spring,
Let them smile as I do now
At the old forsaken bough
   Where I cling.

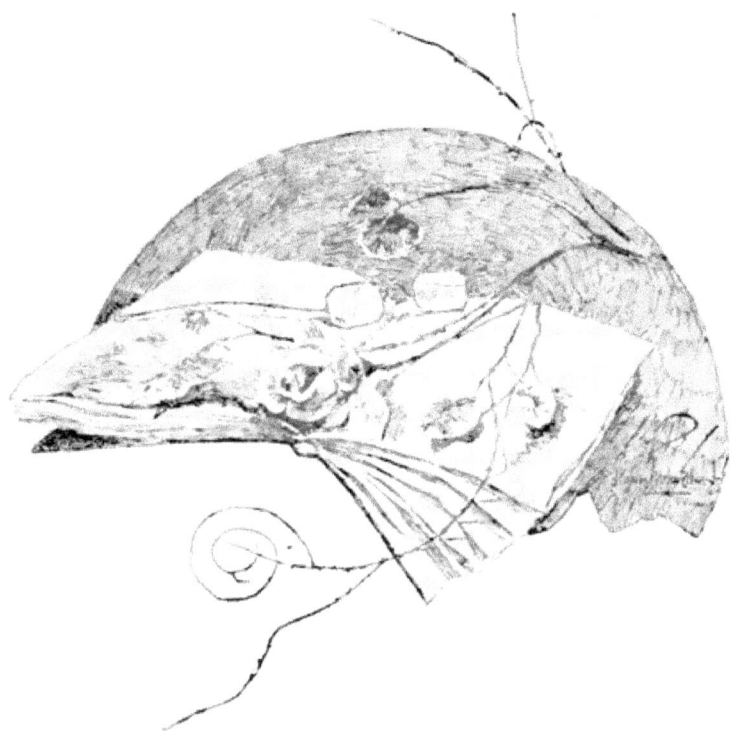

"I saw him once before
As he passed by the door

They say that in his prime
Ere the pruning knife of time
Cut him down.
Not a better Man
Was found —

By the crier on his round
through the town~

Through the town —

But now he walks the streets

— The Streets.

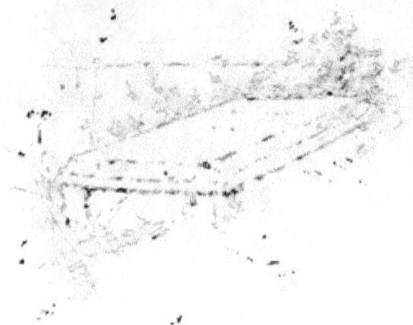

The r... Marbles Rest—

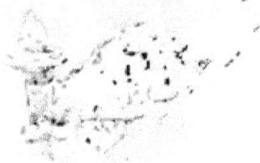

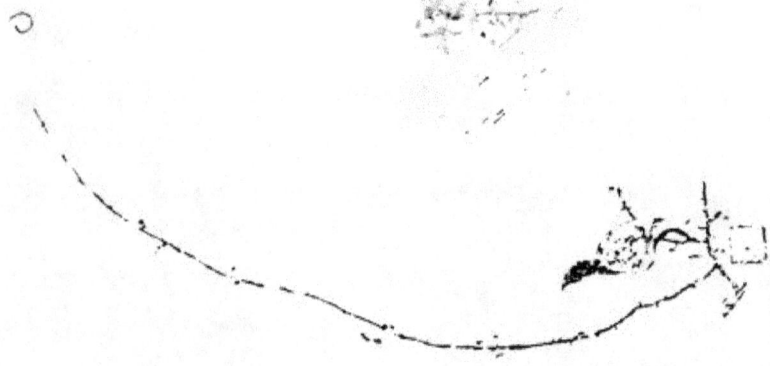

the lips that he
has prest

In their bloom

Patience Ftynpp
Who Departed the
L...

And the names he loved to hear
Have been carved for many a year.
On the tomb.

On the tomb

My Grandmamma has said ·
poor old lady ·
    She is dead long ago ―

like a rose in the snow

"In the snow"

But now his nose & chin
And it rests upon his chin
Like a staff

The old three-cornered hat,
And the breeches, and all that,
Are so queer!

- If I should live to be
    The last leaf upon the tree
        In the Spring. —

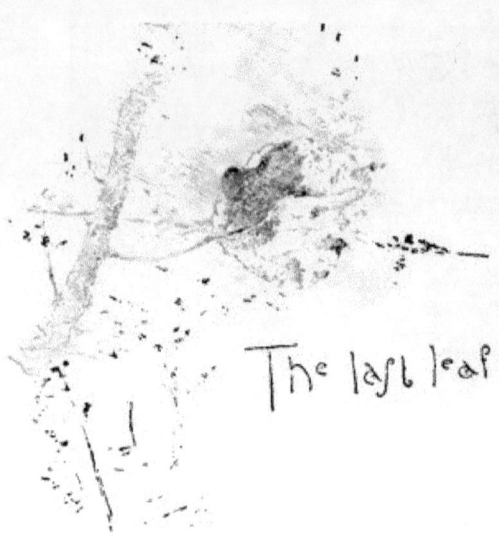

The last leaf upon the tree —

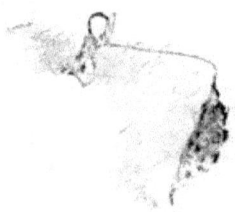

— In the Spring.

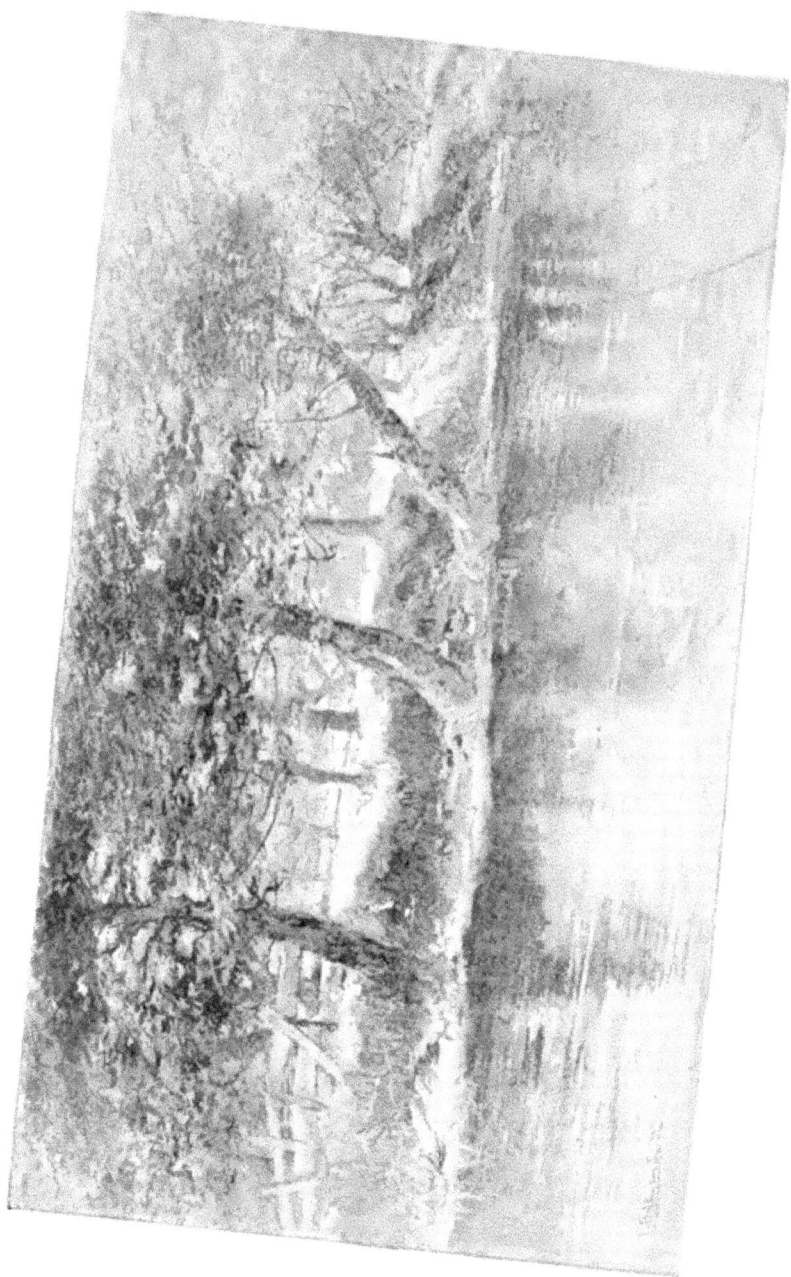

The old forsaken Bough —

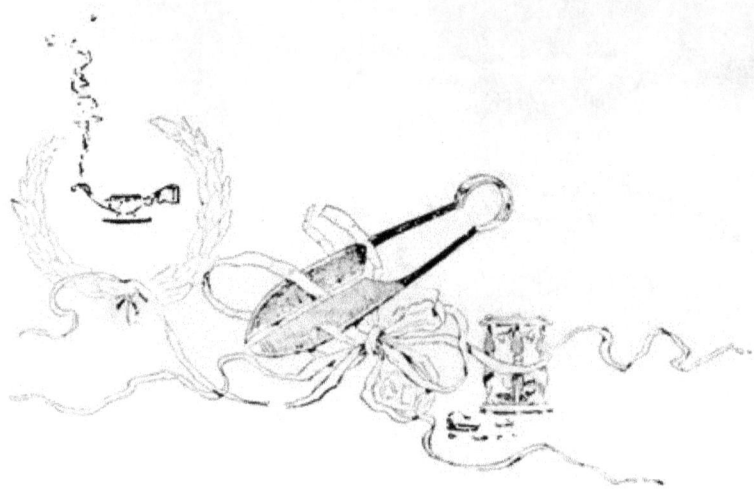

THE
END

The
END

THE HISTORY OF THIS POEM

My publishers tell me that it would add to the interest of the Poem if I would mention any circumstances connected with its composition, publication, and reception. This request must be the excuse of my communicativeness. Just when it was written I cannot exactly say, nor in what paper or periodical it was first published. It must have been written before April, 1833; probably in 1831 or 1832. It was republished in the first edition of my poems, in the year 1836.

The Poem was suggested by the sight of a figure well known to Bostonians of the years just mentioned, that of Major Thomas Melville, "the last of the cocked hats," as he was sometimes called. The Major had been a personable young man, very evidently, and retained evidence of it in

"The monumental pomp of age," —

which had something imposing and something odd about it for youthful eyes like mine. He was often pointed at as one of the "Indians" of the famous "Boston Tea-Party" of 1774. His aspect among the crowds of a later generation reminded me of a withered leaf which has held to its stem through the storms of autumn and winter, and finds itself still clinging to its bough while the new growths of spring are bursting their buds and spreading their foliage all around it. I make this explanation for the benefit of those who have been puzzled by the lines

The last leaf upon the tree
In the Spring.

The way in which it came to be written in a somewhat singular measure was this. I had become a little known as a versifier, and I thought that one or

two other young writers were following my
efforts with imitations, not meant as paro-
dies and hardly to be considered improve-
ments on their models. I determined to
write in a measure which would at once betray
any copyist. So far as it was suggested by any
previous poem, the echo must have come from
Campbell's " Battle of the Baltic," with its short
terminal lines, such as the last of these two,

> By thy wild and stormy steep,
> Elsinore.

But I do not remember any poem in the same measure,
except such as have been written since its publication.

The Poem as first written had one of those false
rhymes which produce a shudder in all educated
persons, even in the Poems of Keats and others
who ought to have known better than to admit them.
The guilty verse ran thus : —

> But now he walks the streets
> And he looks at all he meets
> *So forlorn*,
> And he shakes his feeble head
> That it seems as if he said
> " They are gone ! "

A little more experience, to say nothing of the sneer
of an American critic in an English periodical, showed
me that this would never do. Here was what is called
a " cockney rhyme," — one in which the sound of the
letter *r* is neglected, — maltreated as the letter *h* is
insulted by the average Briton by leaving it out every-
where except where it should be silent. Such an ill-
mated pair as " forlorn " and " gone " could not pos-
sibly pass current in good rhyming society. But what
to do about it was the question. I *must* keep

> " They are gone ! "

and I could not think of any rhyme which I could

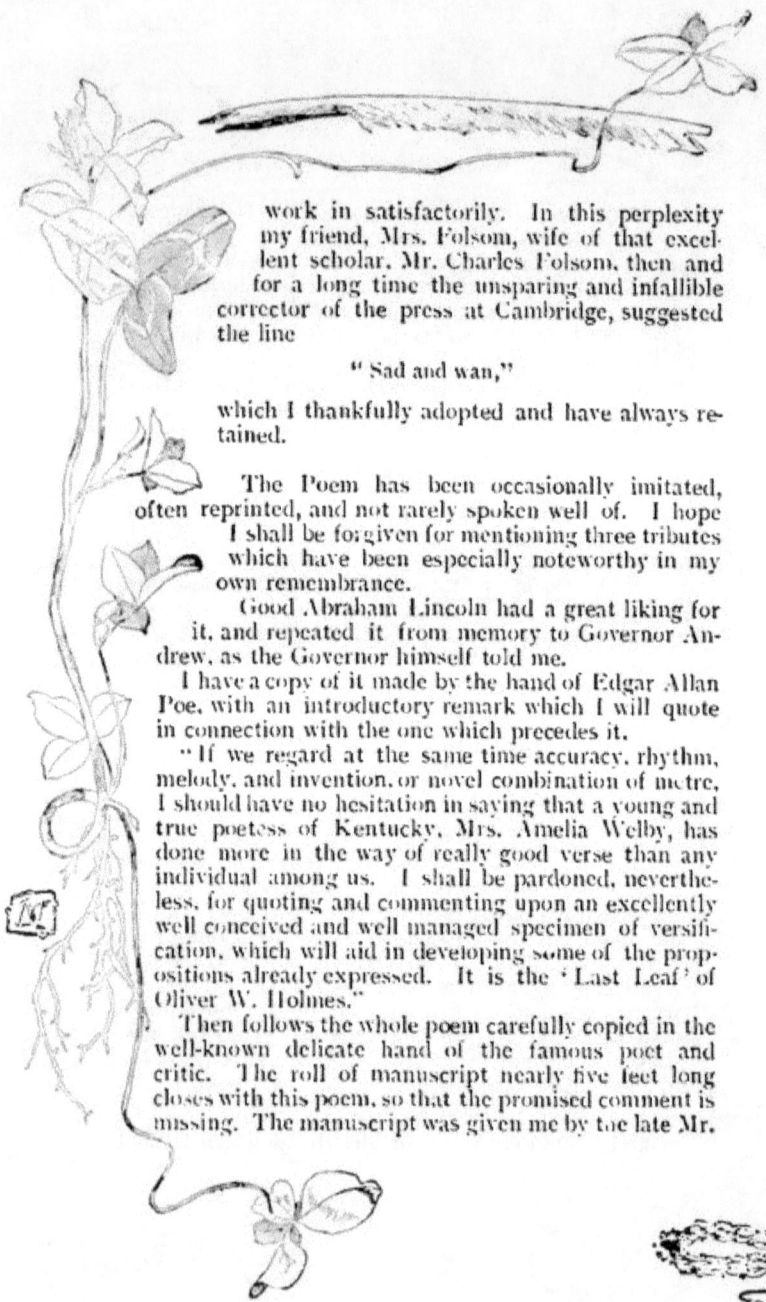

work in satisfactorily. In this perplexity
my friend, Mrs. Folsom, wife of that excel-
lent scholar, Mr. Charles Folsom, then and
for a long time the unsparing and infallible
corrector of the press at Cambridge, suggested
the line

"Sad and wan,"

which I thankfully adopted and have always retained.

The Poem has been occasionally imitated,
often reprinted, and not rarely spoken well of. I hope
I shall be forgiven for mentioning three tributes
which have been especially noteworthy in my
own remembrance.

Good Abraham Lincoln had a great liking for
it, and repeated it from memory to Governor An-
drew, as the Governor himself told me.

I have a copy of it made by the hand of Edgar Allan
Poe, with an introductory remark which I will quote
in connection with the one which precedes it.

"If we regard at the same time accuracy, rhythm,
melody, and invention, or novel combination of metre,
I should have no hesitation in saying that a young and
true poetess of Kentucky, Mrs. Amelia Welby, has
done more in the way of really good verse than any
individual among us. I shall be pardoned, neverthe-
less, for quoting and commenting upon an excellently
well conceived and well managed specimen of versifi-
cation, which will aid in developing some of the prop-
ositions already expressed. It is the 'Last Leaf' of
Oliver W. Holmes."

Then follows the whole poem carefully copied in the
well-known delicate hand of the famous poet and
critic. The roll of manuscript nearly five feet long
closes with this poem, so that the promised comment is
missing. The manuscript was given me by the late Mr.

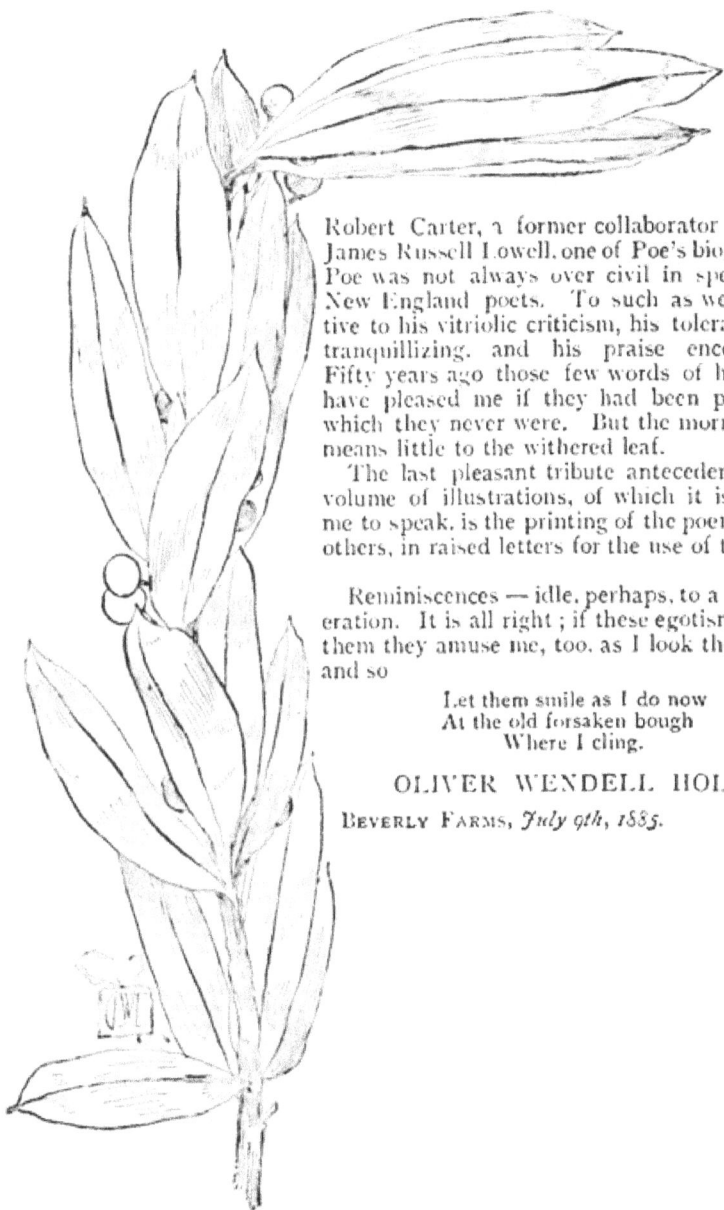

Robert Carter, a former collaborator with Mr.
James Russell Lowell, one of Poe's biographers.
Poe was not always over civil in speaking of
New England poets. To such as were sensi-
tive to his vitriolic criticism, his toleration was
tranquillizing, and his praise encouraging.
Fifty years ago those few words of his would
have pleased me if they had been published,
which they never were. But the morning dew
means little to the withered leaf.

The last pleasant tribute antecedent to this
volume of illustrations, of which it is not for
me to speak, is the printing of the poem, among
others, in raised letters for the use of the blind.

Reminiscences — idle, perhaps, to a new generation. It is all right; if these egotisms amuse
them they amuse me, too, as I look them over;
and so

Let them smile as I do now
At the old forsaken bough
Where I cling.

OLIVER WENDELL HOLMES.

BEVERLY FARMS, *July 9th, 1885.*

PLEASE DO NOT REMOVE
CARDS OR SLIPS FROM THIS POCKET

UNIVERSITY OF TORONTO LIBRARY

www.ingramcontent.com/pod-product-compliance
Lightning Source LLC
Chambersburg PA
CBHW021638270326
41931CB00008B/1067